MULTIPLY
&
DIVIDE

ARMADILLO

1 MULTIPLY ✕

$$0 \times 1 = 0$$
$$1 \times 1 = 1$$
$$2 \times 1 = 2$$
$$3 \times 1 = 3$$
$$4 \times 1 = 4$$
$$5 \times 1 = 5$$
$$6 \times 1 = 6$$
$$7 \times 1 = 7$$
$$8 \times 1 = 8$$
$$9 \times 1 = 9$$
$$10 \times 1 = 10$$
$$11 \times 1 = 11$$
$$12 \times 1 = 12$$

1   DIVIDE ÷

$0 \div 1 = 0$

$1 \div 1 = 1$

$2 \div 1 = 2$

$3 \div 1 = 3$

$4 \div 1 = 4$

$5 \div 1 = 5$

$6 \div 1 = 6$

$7 \div 1 = 7$

$8 \div 1 = 8$

$9 \div 1 = 9$

$10 \div 1 = 10$

$11 \div 1 = 11$

$12 \div 1 = 12$

0	×	2	=	0
1	×	2	=	2
2	×	2	=	4
3	×	2	=	6
4	×	2	=	8
5	×	2	=	10
6	×	2	=	12
7	×	2	=	14
8	×	2	=	16
9	×	2	=	18
10	×	2	=	20
11	×	2	=	22
12	×	2	=	24

$$0 \div 2 = 0$$
$$2 \div 2 = 1$$
$$4 \div 2 = 2$$
$$6 \div 2 = 3$$
$$8 \div 2 = 4$$
$$10 \div 2 = 5$$
$$12 \div 2 = 6$$
$$14 \div 2 = 7$$
$$16 \div 2 = 8$$
$$18 \div 2 = 9$$
$$20 \div 2 = 10$$
$$22 \div 2 = 11$$
$$24 \div 2 = 12$$

0	× 3	=	0
1	× 3	=	3
2	× 3	=	6
3	× 3	=	9
4	× 3	=	12
5	× 3	=	15
6	× 3	=	18
7	× 3	=	21
8	× 3	=	24
9	× 3	=	27
10	× 3	=	30
11	× 3	=	33
12	× 3	=	36

$$0 \div 3 = 0$$
$$3 \div 3 = 1$$
$$6 \div 3 = 2$$
$$9 \div 3 = 3$$
$$12 \div 3 = 4$$
$$15 \div 3 = 5$$
$$18 \div 3 = 6$$
$$21 \div 3 = 7$$
$$24 \div 3 = 8$$
$$27 \div 3 = 9$$
$$30 \div 3 = 10$$
$$33 \div 3 = 11$$
$$36 \div 3 = 12$$

0 × 4 =			0
1 × 4 =			4
2 × 4 =			8
3 × 4 =			12
4 × 4 =			16
5 × 4 =			20
6 × 4 =			24
7 × 4 =			28
8 × 4 =			32
9 × 4 =			36
10 × 4 =			40
11 × 4 =			44
12 × 4 =			48

4 DIVIDE ÷

0	÷	4	=	0
4	÷	4	=	1
8	÷	4	=	2
12	÷	4	=	3
16	÷	4	=	4
20	÷	4	=	5
24	÷	4	=	6
28	÷	4	=	7
32	÷	4	=	8
36	÷	4	=	9
40	÷	4	=	10
44	÷	4	=	11
48	÷	4	=	12

0	×	5	=	0
1	×	5	=	5
2	×	5	=	10
3	×	5	=	15
4	×	5	=	20
5	×	5	=	25
6	×	5	=	30
7	×	5	=	35
8	×	5	=	40
9	×	5	=	45
10	×	5	=	50
11	×	5	=	55
12	×	5	=	60

0	÷	5	=	0
5	÷	5	=	1
10	÷	5	=	2
15	÷	5	=	3
20	÷	5	=	4
25	÷	5	=	5
30	÷	5	=	6
35	÷	5	=	7
40	÷	5	=	8
45	÷	5	=	9
50	÷	5	=	10
55	÷	5	=	11
60	÷	5	=	12

6 MULTIPLY X

$$0 \times 6 = 0$$
$$1 \times 6 = 6$$
$$2 \times 6 = 12$$
$$3 \times 6 = 18$$
$$4 \times 6 = 24$$
$$5 \times 6 = 30$$
$$6 \times 6 = 36$$
$$7 \times 6 = 42$$
$$8 \times 6 = 48$$
$$9 \times 6 = 54$$
$$10 \times 6 = 60$$
$$11 \times 6 = 66$$
$$12 \times 6 = 72$$

$$0 \div 6 = 0$$
$$6 \div 6 = 1$$
$$12 \div 6 = 2$$
$$18 \div 6 = 3$$
$$24 \div 6 = 4$$
$$30 \div 6 = 5$$
$$36 \div 6 = 6$$
$$42 \div 6 = 7$$
$$48 \div 6 = 8$$
$$54 \div 6 = 9$$
$$60 \div 6 = 10$$
$$66 \div 6 = 11$$
$$72 \div 6 = 12$$

7 MULTIPLY ⊗

0	×	7	=	0
1	×	7	=	7
2	×	7	=	14
3	×	7	=	21
4	×	7	=	28
5	×	7	=	35
6	×	7	=	42
7	×	7	=	49
8	×	7	=	56
9	×	7	=	63
10	×	7	=	70
11	×	7	=	77
12	×	7	=	84

7 DIVIDE ÷

0	÷	7	=	0
7	÷	7	=	1
14	÷	7	=	2
21	÷	7	=	3
28	÷	7	=	4
35	÷	7	=	5
42	÷	7	=	6
49	÷	7	=	7
56	÷	7	=	8
63	÷	7	=	9
70	÷	7	=	10
77	÷	7	=	11
84	÷	7	=	12

0	×	8	=	0
1	×	8	=	8
2	×	8	=	16
3	×	8	=	24
4	×	8	=	32
5	×	8	=	40
6	×	8	=	48
7	×	8	=	56
8	×	8	=	64
9	×	8	=	72
10	×	8	=	80
11	×	8	=	88
12	×	8	=	96

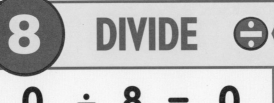

8 DIVIDE ÷

0	÷ 8	=	0
8	÷ 8	=	1
16	÷ 8	=	2
24	÷ 8	=	3
32	÷ 8	=	4
40	÷ 8	=	5
48	÷ 8	=	6
56	÷ 8	=	7
64	÷ 8	=	8
72	÷ 8	=	9
80	÷ 8	=	10
88	÷ 8	=	11
96	÷ 8	=	12

9 MULTIPLY X

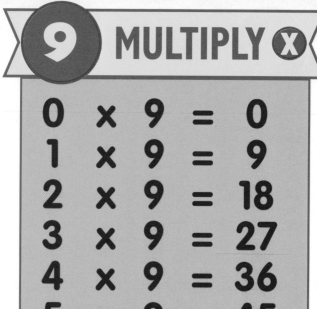

0	× 9	=	0
1	× 9	=	9
2	× 9	=	18
3	× 9	=	27
4	× 9	=	36
5	× 9	=	45
6	× 9	=	54
7	× 9	=	63
8	× 9	=	72
9	× 9	=	81
10	× 9	=	90
11	× 9	=	99
12	× 9	=	108

0	÷ 9	=	0
9	÷ 9	=	1
18	÷ 9	=	2
27	÷ 9	=	3
36	÷ 9	=	4
45	÷ 9	=	5
54	÷ 9	=	6
63	÷ 9	=	7
72	÷ 9	=	8
81	÷ 9	=	9
90	÷ 9	=	10
99	÷ 9	=	11
108	÷ 9	=	12

10 MULTIPLY ✕

0	× 10	=	0
1	× 10	=	10
2	× 10	=	20
3	× 10	=	30
4	× 10	=	40
5	× 10	=	50
6	× 10	=	60
7	× 10	=	70
8	× 10	=	80
9	× 10	=	90
10	× 10	=	100
11	× 10	=	110
12	× 10	=	120

0	÷ 10	=	0
10	÷ 10	=	1
20	÷ 10	=	2
30	÷ 10	=	3
40	÷ 10	=	4
50	÷ 10	=	5
60	÷ 10	=	6
70	÷ 10	=	7
80	÷ 10	=	8
90	÷ 10	=	9
100	÷ 10	=	10
110	÷ 10	=	11
120	÷ 10	=	12

11 MULTIPLY X

$$0 \times 11 = 0$$
$$1 \times 11 = 11$$
$$2 \times 11 = 22$$
$$3 \times 11 = 33$$
$$4 \times 11 = 44$$
$$5 \times 11 = 55$$
$$6 \times 11 = 66$$
$$7 \times 11 = 77$$
$$8 \times 11 = 88$$
$$9 \times 11 = 99$$
$$10 \times 11 = 110$$
$$11 \times 11 = 121$$
$$12 \times 11 = 132$$

$$0 \div 11 = 0$$
$$11 \div 11 = 1$$
$$22 \div 11 = 2$$
$$33 \div 11 = 3$$
$$44 \div 11 = 4$$
$$55 \div 11 = 5$$
$$66 \div 11 = 6$$
$$77 \div 11 = 7$$
$$88 \div 11 = 8$$
$$99 \div 11 = 9$$
$$110 \div 11 = 10$$
$$121 \div 11 = 11$$
$$132 \div 11 = 12$$

0	×	12	=	0
1	×	12	=	12
2	×	12	=	24
3	×	12	=	36
4	×	12	=	48
5	×	12	=	60
6	×	12	=	72
7	×	12	=	84
8	×	12	=	96
9	×	12	=	108
10	×	12	=	120
11	×	12	=	132
12	×	12	=	144

$$0 \div 12 = 0$$
$$12 \div 12 = 1$$
$$24 \div 12 = 2$$
$$36 \div 12 = 3$$
$$48 \div 12 = 4$$
$$60 \div 12 = 5$$
$$72 \div 12 = 6$$
$$84 \div 12 = 7$$
$$96 \div 12 = 8$$
$$108 \div 12 = 9$$
$$120 \div 12 = 10$$
$$132 \div 12 = 11$$
$$144 \div 12 = 12$$

This instant answer number matrix multiplies and divides for you !

For example:
<u>To multiply</u> 7 by 5, first find 7 along the top of the square. Then find 5 down the left side of the square. Run your fingers along each row until they meet. Your total should be 35.
7 x 5 = 35

For example:
<u>To divide</u> 56 by 8, look down the left side of the square to find 8. Then go across this row until you find 56. Lastly go up this row to the top of the square. The number at the top of the row should be 7.
56 ÷ 8 = 7

Use the number matrix to find the answers to these multiplication and division problems:

4 x 5 = ?   6 x 2 = ?   9 x 8 = ?

3 x 9 = ?   7 x 4 = ?   2 x 9 = ?

15 ÷ 3 = ?   42 ÷ 7 = ?   20 ÷ 2 = ?

72 ÷ 9 = ?   63 ÷ 7 = ?   18 ÷ 6 = ?

NUMBER MATRIX

	1	2	3	4	5	6	7	8	9	10	11	12
1	2	3	4	5	6	7	8	9	10	11	12
2	4	6	8	10	12	14	16	18	20	22	24
3	6	9	12	15	18	21	24	27	30	33	36
4	8	12	16	20	24	28	32	36	40	44	48
5	10	15	20	25	30	35	40	45	50	55	60
6	12	18	24	30	36	42	48	54	60	66	72
7	14	21	28	35	42	49	56	63	70	77	84
8	16	24	32	40	48	56	64	72	80	88	96
9	18	27	36	45	54	63	72	81	90	99	108
10	20	30	40	50	60	70	80	90	100	110	120
11	22	33	44	55	66	77	88	99	110	121	132
12	24	36	48	60	72	84	96	108	120	132	144

First published 2000 by Armadillo Books
An imprint of Bookmart Limited
Desford Road, Enderby
Leicester LE9 5AD
England

ISBN 1-90046-648-1

Printed in Spain